COMPASS ION Book Series

ALL THINGS YOU

A Unique Approach To The Enlightenment
Of Yourself As All Things

FAITH BOUIE

Copyright © 2019 **Faith Bouie**

All rights reserved. This book or parts thereof may not be reproduced in any form, stored in any retrieval system, or transmitted in any form by any means—electronic, mechanical, photocopy, recording, or otherwise—without prior written permission of the publisher, except as provided by United States of America copyright law. For permission requests, write to the publisher, at "Attention: Permissions Coordinator," at the provided web address below.

Cover design by Fiverr Cover Designer, Germancreative. Copyediting by Sam Wright.

ISBN: 978-1-7342128-0-8 (Ebook)
ISBN: 978-1-7342128-1-5 (Paperback)

This book is dedicated to my father Sam, as a very special thank you for being such a powerful spiritual influence in my life.

Contents

A Very Brief Introduction 1

Chapter 1: You Are Everything That You See 5

Chapter 2: How To Perceive Everything As You 15

Chapter 3: How Life Communicates Expressions Of You 27

Chapter 4: A Brief Note On Thought Addiction 39

Chapter 5: Watching All As You Heals You 53

Chapter 6: COMPASS ION - An Introduction To Conscious Meditation 61

Chapter 7: Conscious Meditation 75

About The Author 81

A Very Brief Introduction

September 19, 2019
Bradenton, FL

I awakened my ability to channel during my studies as a student in hypnotherapy school in 2015. It came about quite naturally as I studied altered states of mind and consciousness. Subsequently, it became an evolved gift that I have truly learned to cherish over time.

During the eight-month training as a hypnotherapist, accessing altered states of mind became an effortless task to facilitate within myself the more exposure that I had to the school's curriculum and teachings. And during this time, I channeled a large body of work within a total of five months. My work was channeled from my own inner source with the grace and guided generosity of several entities. Much of what I've channeled was achieved in deep meditation with much resemblance to the ancient teachings we read about today. However, what I have found along my own personal journey is this knowledge is never lost. It is only transmuted into another face of comprehension as the human evolves in what we acknowledge as time.

***

This book represents only one of the various principles channeled from those days, and it is a very cherished philosophy which I am now learning to honor more every day.

You are everything that you see as you consciously perceive this waking reality, and every notion, thing and every person you make acquaintance with, day to day, is honorably you in truth.

There is only The One who is having This Experience. As one opens herself to this very concept, compassion can thus be truly born into presence, and she can acknowledge the suffering *and* the happiness of others as her own.

Peace is born from the stillness of what is transmuted from within the heart as she honors life anew in the absence of judgment and place.

***

This is the very first teaching that surfaced into consciousness while I was in a deeply altered state of mind. My intentions are for this book to provide a guided step-by-step comprehension of what it truly means to live your life consciously and compassionately in honor of the self that you are within all things, so hidden as it may seem.

I have not channeled what we are about to delve into at this time. May our journey together through this teaching be of much joy and enlightenment for *the all* of us.

Namasté

Chapter I

YOU ARE EVERYTHING THAT YOU SEE

September 21st, 2019

Y*ou are everything that you see.* What does this mean? It is certainly a very demanding notion to digest. Since the dawning of childhood, we have instilled and embedded within us various subsets of separation which we have learned to appreciate over time. We honor the strong value in principles such as selection, comparison, and subject isolation. And we have found much purpose (and comfort) in the notion that I am me, and *you* are you.

So, if I were to suggest to you that you *are* me and that you are too, every possible conceivable thing that exists within this waking reality which you call life, how would this make you feel?

For some, perhaps it would more than likely become an impossible task to entertain because you simply wouldn't know *how* to consider this notion or *where* to begin. Identity consciousness attempts to reconcile with that which is being said; however, a strong hierarchy of the self along with self-perception quickly overrides and discards this concept with little to no effort at all.

This is a very beautiful and quite natural process of the mind.

***

In hypnotherapy school, I learned of an aspect of the conscious mind capable of rejecting incoming suggestions conflicting to the nature of the client's current thought regimen. It is known as the Critical Factor of the conscious mind, and it will allow certain information only into the subconscious mind that is within resonance with what feels true for the person. I have always acknowledged it as the ultimate semipermeable membranous gateway seated at the entry of the subconscious mind, permitting only what is conducive to the current system of thinking embedded within subconsciousness.

***

And so, notions such as *you are not this, and you are not that* are words which ring very true and harmoniously for many people, as we rely on what *we are not* to tell us what we truly are.

If I am not this, then I am that. *I am not beautiful; therefore, I am ugly. I am not an animal, I am a human being. I am not black, nor am I Hispanic; I am white. I am not rich; therefore, I am poor. I am not happy, I am sad. I am not healthy, I am sick. I am not you, I am me.* And for those of us who acknowledge spiritual themes, *I am not me, I am. I am not human, I am pure consciousness, and I am Spirit.*

Quite frankly, it sounds like the process of elimination to me. According to this model, you are *by process of elimination* what you are. And yet, what if there coexisted another mean of comprehending what you truly are in great reference to your life and reality as you know it?

What if you were all and everything that you see and experience from day-to-day? How would this change how that you feel about the things that you see and come into contact within your life? What if in truth, *the you* who I am referencing is truly The One incarnate sentient being subsisting within all things seen and unseen upon all levels of dimension simultaneously? What if you were the pure embodiment of all that is? What if you were God manifested as the One Experience?

***

I wonder how this would change the concepts of love and compassion. To see all before you as you can no longer rely heavily upon notions such as sympathy in the light of pain and suffering.

When we see others as ourselves truly, old aphorisms such as *"Treat others the ways in which you would like to be treated"*, become a reality lived in complete vindication of that truth, and can no longer remain outlined as a preference of choice contingent to the individual's principles of morality.

***

To acknowledge everything within and outside of you as you is equivalent to acknowledging the entirety of that which you truly are. You are an all-encompassing multidimensional being, and you are truly beautiful in every respect of this honor and acknowledgment.

***

Quite naturally, the initial fear that you are also the "ugliness" perceived within this world, could more than likely cause much controversy and strife from deep within the self simply because to know the beauty of this world is to also acknowledge the pain that comes with it.

Perchance you may even reject this notion alone for the sake of not being the very things which you've conditioned yourself to resent and/or fear all of your life. If it would bring you temporary comfort to know these things are not you, perhaps you may feel it is just to do so.

Be that as it may, to see and acknowledge all things as you paradoxically grants you the freedom from all pain and suffering, which will be discussed later.

***

You are free without limits set to that which you are, and you are the sentient being having the one experience upon many shapes and many forms of expression.

However, the journey doesn't end with the knowledge that you are all things. It is remarkably only the beginning of a very profound journey into the greatest comprehension of one's self. As we acknowledge the very things in our surrounding reality as who we are truly, a game is born in the place of isolation and separation. It is a game which honors the marvels of potential energy and consciousness splayed into various customs and faces of expression. It is a game born from the source of that which you are, founded in the present, here and the now. It is a game that suggests that you are the very words that you are reading at this very moment displayed upon the computer screen (or book).

How you feel in sentiment and deep reflection of this notion thus becomes the play of the game.

Stillness becomes a true practice as consciousness acknowledges the many expressions of consciousness. And as this unfolds, messages that were once buried in subconsciousness, hidden and unseen, are now revealed to you in the greatest, most profound ways imaginable. Energy is no longer harbored, and can thus be transmuted and released to the source from which it came as one evolves into the truest and utmost embodiment of wholeness.

Let us journey together into the greatest comprehension of one's self as all things.

Namasté

Chapter II

How To Perceive Everything As You

September 23rd, 2019

We perceive our world through our senses as our senses unfold our world to us. What is more, our senses can tell us a lot about how we choose to filter our world, as we map our perceptions out unto reality in the countless attempts of riddling the ruse we acknowledge as life.

And thus, our journey begins with this simple question: *How do you perceive you?*

A very vital question that is addressed in how you perceive yourself *now* will shape how life (you) communicates to you along this journey and discovery of yourself within all things.

***

Life is built upon many thought-forms, and what you perceive as *time* are ripples of these very thought-forms lengthened and delayed into the various expressions of who you are. Life thus becomes, in this respect, the ultimate expression of you, *and you*, the very expression of life itself.

The question is now: *Who are you?* This is not the very commonly known question that so many of us have entertained within the context of esoteric themes and spiritual bewilderment. It is a simple rhetorical question delivered from an awareness, unfiltered by separation and duality.

And so as follows, a response that, *I do not know who I am, serves* as the earliest stepping stones of wisdom in the great discovery of self in all things. Subconscious reflex ceases to function through the default of old and stubborn paradigms, as a brief respite is born from the surrender of not knowing for the moment. The mind is at rest in this way which causes you to be ever more present to the question that was just asked to you.

You already knew who you were the moment I asked the question in the absence of mind. It was proposed in a Socratic fashion for the reason of bringing forth consciousness in an identifiable way to you, as you gradually learn to observe your consciousness among the many things around you.

***

In the absence of mind, life is voided of all mental expression as pure consciousness can thus be felt upon the plane in subtle, yet overwhelming expressions of peace, joy, and bliss. This is true spiritualism for the many of us who have experienced such beauty, and it is certainly an undeniable ecstasy to achieve.

With that being said, it is not without thought are we capable of navigating our everyday physical lives because consciousness without mind poses a direct contradiction to the order of incarnation and how things are naturally manifested into physical expression.

We commonly acknowledge ego identity as the mental impression of self through means of various thought-form expressions such as, *I am happy* and/or *I am sad.* However, we never stop to think, *What is happy?* And moreover, *What is this thing I call sad?* I address these questions as though I were a child learning to feel her emotions for the very first time. And from this approach, I ask in all great sincerity within regards to the direct experience. What is soon discovered is that you are the very thing which you call sadness. And you are happiness too, as well. You are the expression of both vibrations, and so too are you the space from which they came. You are the garden and the gardener, as you have nurtured their tiny seeds into fruition.

In truth, you are that which exists prior to the arrival of thought-forms, as pure and complete expression. And in response to this, thought operates as the by-product, secondary to that which was already there from the very beginning: *you.*

Toiling within an eternal movement of expression upon itself, *like* is capable of attracting the *like-wise* in an endless continuum of energy. The breach of this energy unto physical incarnation is what is *the acknowledgment of life.*

***

How do you perceive everything as you? This is where I teach you how to perceive *you.* You are the window. You are the door. You are the ceiling. You are the floor.

My question now is: *Did you look at the window, door, ceiling, and floor upon reading the latter passage?* If so, *how did it make you feel?* Perhaps, a distant and foreign recognition and appreciation for what was there overcame you. Or perhaps, you felt nothing at all. Perhaps, you were accompanied by thought vibrations and/or feelings of fear, regret, anger or sadness. Or perhaps you felt nothing at all. Perchance you even felt physical sensations from within the body. This would be true, for *all* is an expression of *you.*

If we were to dissect each sentence, it is possible to acknowledge that *you are*, that *you are*. This is truth. However, the disconnect lies in the initial reflex to deny each subject noun its place in this truth as well. A subtle sense of subjugation settles within the mind, as it attempts to deduct from what is an inseparable aspect to the entirety of you.

The label of that which stands in expression as *the door* is not the door. You are the expression of what is known *as door* before thought arrives at this conclusion. A very strange yet familiar recognition to that which you are can be realized as you unmask the masquerade in discovery to what has been temporarily forgotten.

***

You are the things in which you see. To initiate this recognition process, the very first thing that you must do is release the idea that you *are not* the things that you are seeing. This is pivotal in the greater scheme of recognition because *as you are not something*, you are in complete rejection of an aspect of yourself which subsists on subtler planes of perception, consequently, causing conflict and dissonance from within. It is important to remember that *you are* what *you are* prior to the assimilation of thought programs when watching the things around you. This will bring forth a sense of neutrality, as consciousness can thus participate within itself once more.

✳✳✳

The later phenomenon which follows as you perceive your reality as yourself truly is the emergence of *Compass Ion*, which will be discussed at a later time in this book. With the utmost significance and grace from deep within the eternal depths of your being, *Compass Ion* represents the oldest source of wisdom known to man, and it serves as your ultimate guide and very source of recognition along your surrender to true perception.

Let's say that you were to choose a word upon this screen (or book) to focus upon. The first thing that you'll want to do is release the idea that this word *is not* you. To do this, perhaps you may suggest to yourself simply the possibility of there being something more to *this word* you are willing to entertain. The simple acknowledgment *that the word is here*, would suffice alone, as it provides the absence of judgment in its place.

The achievement of the latter step unlocks the passage to recognition, and you are thus ready to receive the message that is there.

***

CHAPTER DISCUSSION & PRACTICE

How do you perceive you? Take time to reflect on this question as you ponder some of the most common things you conclude about yourself throughout your day. Great insight can be gained in how ego builds and presents a case file to you of the many things which are agreeable and *disagreeable* in respect to how you regard yourself as a person and human being. As you allow these impressions to surface into consciousness reflect on how they make you feel.

EXERCISE - I Am *Object*

Take an object near you at this time and sit it in front of you. Notice any thoughts that may surface to consciousness as you sit in observation of this object. Once the thoughts have finally settled, welcome the idea that this object is you and notice the very first feelings to emerge as you do so. Try your very best to release all predispositions surrounding the notion that this object is not you. Simply acknowledge that it is there and that it is undeniably you in every regard, allowing space for consciousness to observe itself. You may notice that more is perceptible as you observe with a much more expanded regard for what is there.

Chapter III

How Life Communicates Expressions Of You

September 26th, 2019

You are a direct expression of life itself, as life communicates to you the very expressions of you in the many impressions, people, places and things which you see every day-to-day. And it is when you live your life in awareness to what you see, are you capable of unraveling the truth of what is truly there beneath.

Center yourself to the very moment now, as you bring awareness to the world around you. This is the very first ruse of you: *the very notion there is a world that surrounds you.* Although this may seem as rightfully so, the world is actually you, and you are the *world*. You are the tree, and you are its leaves. You are a human being. And so too are you the air amidst all things.

***

Love acknowledges love in the greatest form of compassion when you are able to decipher the divine encryption of all things as you. What is more, you are free to navigate your concept of what is perceived as *world* with profound wisdom and responsibility in respects to the greater entirety and honor of you.

After the releasement of the belief that something *is not* you, the awakening of this communication unto your reality can be perceived. And as this unfolds, are you able to stand in recognition to that which is beckoning your decryption and reception. It is a constant reconciliation concerning *that which you are* and *that which you are becoming.* That is why you perceive this energy reconciliation in what may seem like different people, places, thoughts, and experiences. In essence, what you are experiencing are the many reconciliations of you (conscious energy) encrypted into many faces and expressions of energy, as so hidden as it may seem. It is a beautiful process, as light filters unto the plane in the various expressions of light.

Light consciousness serves as the very premise to what you essentially are. And it is your unique interpretation of how you choose to perceive your reality which serves as the very reflection and interpretation of what is perceived as yourself in consideration you are all light consciousness. Therefore, it is the everso subtle insinuation that *something is not you* which defeats this very purpose and entry of the discovery of self as all things.

***

THE INNOCENCE OF MIND

Ego identifies itself amongst the many things that it deems "identifiable". What is more, it finds much enjoyment in the role it plays in the continual deciphering of what is pragmatic in respects to what is of somatic regard, as it regurgitates upon itself recycled thought programs which lie dormant within subconsciousness in the various struggles of re-creating that which it is naturally incapable of fully comprehending.

True and refined frustrations of *mind* such as these go unbeknownst to you. For how can your mind ever communicate to you it *does not truly understand* what it is seeing? It doesn't for that matter for mind doesn't understand *that it doesn't understand.* This is an inconceivable notion for the mind to grasp. It thrives within its own set principles of function, as it re-creates what is happening before your eyes via internal interpretations of recycled thought-forms which emerge into consciousness. Mind is all the more so incapable of conceding anything outside of what it has always been. The innocence of mind thus poses as a beautiful lesson upon the journey and discovery of all things *you.*

***

Mind serves as a parable to what you are regarding how you choose to participate in what you perceive as *world.* You are your mind, and you are your thoughts, feelings, and emotions. Everything that you see is you in disguise, and so too does this philosophy apply to what manifests inside the mind. As mind filters upon your reality, it labels *what is what* as you immerse yourself in the entertainment of what is happening. Be that sadness or fear and/or happiness and cheer, mind tells you what is happening as you internally consent to what you perceive to be real.

Life serves as a fable for the self-enlightenment of light consciousness upon the physical plane, and the various impressions of mind that are perceived as thought, emotions and feelings coexist as the colors in the very rainbow *you are* in this fairytale. Light is of all things magical and seemingly unmagical. And it is with great courage are you able to surrender to the truth that all things are really you.

As you consent to this notion, another dimension of perception opens itself to you, as the gestalt of mind commences within appropriate means and reflection to what it truly is, providing you with proper feedback that is coherent to the utmost philosophy of all things as you.

***

THE WISDOM OF OTHERS AS YOURSELF

You are the very people in which you see. In childhood, you could probably remember what it was like to sit on the swing, as you watched as others on the playground had fun and played. Perchance you could even recall the gossip from those very many years ago. Such memories of *how the bully named Timmy was always such a very "bad" and "disruptive" kid in school*, as well as, *how Sarah was always so "quiet" and so very "different" than you and the others in your class.*

Bad, disruptive, quiet and *different* are a part of life's numerous efforts to communicate to you something regarding yourself in truth as light consciousness, and so too were the children from those earlier days. It is a beautiful honor to acknowledge life in this respect as it spills forth upon the plane in various impressions of light expression. You are light, and so too are those you may have understood as *"others"* to you.

***

Seeing another, you identify them by their skin, color, shape, and size among many other things, as you create pairing deductions with the intent of justifying who they are *whilst* justifying *who you are not*. This can be very, very limiting and quite preposterous in respects to the magnificent, all-encompassing nature of what you *truly* are.

Understand that seeing others coupled with their actions and corresponding behaviors, as yourself truly, will not *dim* the light that you are by any means, and if anything, it would brighten it even more within high regards to the compassion which is born in acknowledgment of this acceptance.

Peace lies within the great honor and highest regard to suffering. It's magically paradoxical and sacred in respects to the individual who harnesses its wisdom with much truth and understanding.

It is *you* who is realized the minute you see unto others with your eyes, and to wield this gift is to understand the multi-faceted nature of what you truthfully are upon many other dimensions of being as you play in context to what you perceive as reality. Quality of perception is thus improved tenfold, as your awareness expands beyond the confinements and focus of solely *self*, and you are blessed with the compassionate perspective and comprehension of the lives lived by others. It is an unfortunate mistake *not* to deem these lives as your own, for to do this robs you of your conscious expansion upon the physical realm of this world.

***

Many spiritualists have led their lives in opposition to many of the notions brought forth in the teachings which I speak of in this channeling, as it is not deemed *wise* to acknowledge mental structures and the things of this reality as yourself. It is commonly understood by many mystics that you *are not* your body, nor are you *by any means* mind and ego. *You are the utter purity of consciousness and that is all.* It is my purpose to tell you that *you are* the very things I speak of *and much more.* I stand in no opposition to the fact that you are the utmost embodiment of perfection, and that you are consciousness. However, it is not my place to tell you *what you are not,* for it is believed that you are *all* things.

Much wisdom and beauty can be found in the incarnation of consciousness into physical form and vibration. As this energetic bond is fortified on much subtler planes of reality, *vibration becomes the very heart of consciousness, as consciousness becomes the very heart of vibration* in the most essential dance of physical expression. Consequently, our physical world consists of very dense and heavy energetic fields of vibration. And yet, it is the unanimity-consciousness of *all things as you* which collapses the various cemented impressions of separation set upon physical perception as consciousness observes itself as all things, and life becomes a playground for spiritual freedom and enlightenment.

Chapter IV

A Brief Note On Thought Addiction

August 23rd, 2017

There is a great possibility that the thoughts which presently occupy your mind at this time all derive from old and obsolete systems of thinking which have outlived their purpose, as the expansion of who you are truly now unfolds in the yearning conscious consent to know yourself beyond how you've come to know yourself thus far in your waking life. What is more, a large majority of the thoughts that are held at this time may more than likely originate from the regurgitation of the past facets of derivative thinking and are therefore not truly from any absolute or direct resource.

The truth of who you are *precedes* The Thought. And to come into the knowledge of that which you truly are in this very moment, you must come to know in truth what essentially precedes *The Thought*.

So, who are you then? *Are you this thought of you now?* Or are you the thoughts of *who you were* just a few moments ago? Whatever the answer may be, I leave for you to decide. This decision has always been made from the perspective of thought; however, as you acknowledge the nature of *that which surrounds the rising thought*, much more will reveal itself to you, for the very truth of you lies *beyond and before* the thought ever manifested, as it serves as the very truth and veracity of you and what it truly means to be human.

***

Thoughts have become everyday habits in our lives in our ongoing discernment of reality. They govern how we act and how we feel, and everything that we do *turns over in direct response to the next rising thought.*

What you are lies beyond the nature of your thinking, while the very nature of your thinking proves to be otherwise. *What is it about thinking which haunts us? And why is it so addictive? Why do we find it so easy to lose ourselves so willingly in a sea of our own thinking?* Moreover, why do we find it *so easy* to do so? Why do we choose to think and relate to a thing which has already transpired and/or is unfolding in the very moment so easily and readily before ever having the chance to *fully embrace the experience* firsthand?

***

It's our very nature to associate ourselves with our thoughts. We, therefore, experience our lives through solely our thinking. And as life happens, we are ever more so inclined to think simultaneously as the experience unfolds without ever consciously experiencing it. It is not to say that this is wrong by any means. However, it is believed to be truly retrograde in the order in which life unfolds.

Thoughts are only a common by-product of the reality in which we experience. What is more, they play a major role in how we feel and how we emote the emotions that are thereby influenced by the very thoughts in which we think day-to-day. By sending vibrations throughout various areas within our human vessels, the emission of these emotions and feelings are the usual result. In the order in which life transpires, The Thought is not *the only* solution in the Soul's great analysis and desire to know life; it is only the result from the very sustenance of what is unfolding *at the moment.* Likewise, emotions and feelings are of the same very nature and yet, they too are found to be very addictive in our daily interaction with life.

***

Life is truly sacred and is believed to be a gift of sacred practice.

"Life happens to the human" is what the mind tells us to protect us often. However, as we move before the mind ever speaks, we learn that Life *is* the human, and we can appreciate the human form as that of an apparatus for the primary function of experiencing life through physical interpretation and form; and moreover in a likewise expression, we can acknowledge *thoughts*, *emotions*, and *feelings* as common features too very important in the nature they are processed and respected.

***

When we invest in how we feel and think before life ever has a chance of unfolding naturally, we trap ourselves in a tsunami of illusion, like that of an energetic pull and suction. It's the expansive nature of thought which makes it so addictive. Thought being an *"easy-fix"* of resolution to what is happening at the moment, that is. Logic, therefore, becomes a treat *to treat* the unknown. And life grows seemingly more predictable as one continuously vibrates and emits vibrations that constitute what is predictable for that human.

When you expose this pattern, you essentially expose the truth of why we think so much. *What is that truth for you?* Anything in excess serves only a need that will never be filled because for it to be in excess can only mean it was not being adequately filled in the very first place.

***

Perchance it may seem as quite a burden to let go of what you've known all your life in the patterns in which you think. It's certainly no easy task. However, when you make the shift into other means of processing as you discern reality, what was initially perceived as an impossible task will turn into a natural habit as it serves the truth and very nature of human design.

Multidimensional processing expands the consciousness of you, and therefore, satisfies the hunger to *"know"* and/or *"understand"* the reality in which you seek comfort. Thoughts will serve as a multitude of this awakening as you create this shift and will be more abundant by nature.

What is more, as you come to understand the nature of what exists beyond thinking, you free yourself from the shackles of thinking so obsessively. You are designed to know what lies here before you *before* you come to know it within your natural, waking state of consciousness. It couldn't exist any possible other way, for you are *beyond* The Thought, and so too are you the Thought. Therefore, your will *to know* too lies beyond what is known in the present, and what is known can therefore only become known to you as you simply *allow* what is there to *simply be* as *is*.

Your very design as a human being coupled with consciousness splayed into form enables you the means of reaction and interaction with your environment in ways that satisfy your thinking. It is habitual thought which binds us to more obsessive thinking. And yet, it is believed that as life truly unfolds are you to question if you *are simply reacting* or actually *interacting* with life as it transpires.

As he thinks, so doeth he needs.

Thinking derives from a place of need which is born within the presence of thought and the *absence* of one's experience of life, making people ever more inclined to *think* about their experiences without ever truly experiencing them. As one fails to feel what they see, they misinterpret the actual thing in front of them as *what was thought* during the time of the experience. This causes an interruption in the natural processing of life, as the individual leads a life carried solely in thought.

This is where I tell you why you think so much.
   One word: *Unknown.*

Life is unknown, and it is very much so an illusion created by the mind to believe that it is so predictable. Mind carries thoughts throughout great millennia of experiences to provide comfort to the discomfort *of not knowing* what will happen next; therefore, your relationship to *what is unknown* becomes your way of life.

Behind your thought conditioning lies someone who yearns to simply *know*. Beyond this desire *to know*, however, lies a *you* who has *already seen*. And yet it is here, where your desire *to know* overpowers the *you who already knows*.

It is for this very reason, *as life happens are we to happen along with it* because it is when you finally release this desire to know, are you properly aligned to that which is *already known*.

You *are* life. And your human specimen serves as an extension of this very truth.

Swirling in a mist of your own thinking inhibits life from unfolding organically through you. It's not happening *to* you; thoughts relating to *more* thoughts about life's many happenings *create the habit of relation*, thus feeding the illusion this is so.

Relatability proves to be a powerful force to overcome, as we are inclined to relate to almost everything that crosses our path as it serves as a fairly common solution to most experiences that take place before us.

You are reading these words while two of the following are taking place. You are relating simultaneously to what you've come to know in relation to what is read while processing what is there before you. The question is now, *"Are you actually reading these words or are you relating what is being read to something from another time?"*.

FAITH BOUIE

Relation is a fickle beast for the only way for you to truly answer this question is to observe the actions of your mind in retrospect, *after* you've related the experience to another notion.

To relate to something is to give meaning to a thing that has no meaning, therefore, subsiding under the processes of your own past functioning with the intentions of those very ideas serving in proper representation of what is here now before you.

***

A cat is a cat. However, the notion of a cat is imbedded now and forever within you until you decide that *it is not.* And therefore, every cat that crosses your path will present as so until you come to understand that they are truly not cats at all, nor are they the temporary label which you've regurgitated upon them, but *much, much more.*

Knowing that *a cat is a cat* satisfies your mind for the moment, for to know something is a seed planted in soil, as the mind hungers to process what it *does not know*. This is because the mind is being improperly used. *An improper tool functions overtime to satisfy what is being beckoned to be satisfied.* From a place of lack and from a need to know thus starves the mind and prompts it to behave in such a manner.

To that regard, it is believed that the tool of the mind is to function in a much more organic respect. And life can therefore naturally unfold and operate through that of an expansive and limitless mind, a beautiful process to witness, as one sets aside himself *to live*, and therefore release control.

Chapter V

WATCHING ALL AS YOU HEALS YOU

September 30th, 2019

You were very young, at the very beginning of your life when you were instilled with the words, *"He, she, it, they, you, her, we* and *I"*. Perchance your elders would have shown you differently during those earlier and very magical years of wonderment, *how would this shape your reality as you understand it today?* How differently would you be now if you were taught from a very young age that the other little boys and girls in your school who you learned and played with every day were truthfully you *in disguise?* What if you understood perhaps at a very early age that what you perceived as *"we"*, was the *one and only* consciousness dispersed into various forms of unique expression, *and that all was weaved from the very same cloth and fabrication of conscious life?* How different would you be today if you heard *those words* back then when you were ever so young in tandem with a mind like that of a *sponge*, ripe and ready for knowledge? I wonder how differently your decisions would have transpired up until this very moment if you acknowledged every human, morsel, animal, object and/or notion as that of your own in all sincerity. If you were to acknowledge me as yourself truly at this time whilst your eyes process the words which are being read, how could this change your entire outlook on the life which you acknowledge as *life? Who* would you be in that regard if you knew the things that you now know?

***

PROFOUND CONSCIOUSNESS

You are me and everything else, *seen and unseen*. This is because you are much, much more than *I* and/or *we*. You are *all*. And this is the true beauty of *you*.

Hence, you are the very words that are being read at this time, and so too are you the very device by which they are held to display. You are the sounds of grumbling from within your belly when you are hungry, and so too are you *the hunger*. You are the emotions of anger which surface in the heat of conflict and disagreement, and so too are you the very face of that which follows when all have settled. You are the peace in the world and so too are you the wars which take place. As you are life, so too are you *death*. And as you are the many hues of bliss and goodness, so too are you the various expressions of hate and disgust. You are everything, whilst you are nothing at all. You are me, *and I,* you.

To that notion is consciousness born from the grace and wisdom of ignorance as you are thus *this* beautiful.

Profound consciousness begets the premise for healing within the individual as he embraces a life abundant with compassionate regard for the features present in his reality.

You are hidden within the very seams of reality.

You are the old, and you are the new. You are the coming, and you are the going. You are never one thing alone. You are in constant motion, like that of flowing water. And notions such as pain and suffering follow this very same principle. However, if for any reason are you ever subsided to *one pain,* then so be it, *it shall be the very truth of you until you agree otherwise.* It is through the means of personal choice and principle are we ever cemented within our suffering. What is more, stubbornness held to solely one frequency and *one way* alone could be very limiting for the one who is *limitless.*

And thus, it is when we are in agreement with what surrounds us, are we able to hold a compassionate gaze to reality with great awareness to who we truly are. And if there is ever any *pain*, we can thus acknowledge it as ourselves truly with profound honor to that regard without hesitation. And with this, *how it transpired* will no longer turn into a great mystery to be solved. Instead, what springs forth in its place becomes a message that is immediately processed at the very time of origination. Truth is always ever so effortless in this respect.

What is more, this phenomenon bridges the consciousness with *what was so seemingly subconscious to you before,* as trust between the two minds are bonded in agreement to the reality held before them and are grounded within the faculties of the present and the now.

***

Healing begins as one ends the notion of separation regarding *self* within respects to *all things.* The great gestalt of all things as yourself truly regards the hidden facets of you contained within your *memories, beliefs,* and *emotions* about the world, as it molds the collection of your inner-world coupled with your mirrored outer-world into *one conscious regard.* And as osmosis things are thus unanimous, free and true, given this acknowledgment.

Do not fear pain for pain is concealed truth that can be easily removed just as quickly as it came. *It is but an expression of you truly.* In ignorance, it only grows. Likewise, any traces of indifference born from this regard would only acknowledge it as *a separate entity from what you are,* feeding the hungry belly of its fire even more.

In expression, it yearns for your sole recognition as you rest in profound regard to its *choice in expression,* then allowing its course of energy to properly flow in *and out* of you as initially intended for it to be.

This message is not, *by any means,* to be translated into the suggestion of not seeking medical attention when medically necessary. It is yet a message surrounding the wisdom understood through the means of consciousness in the presence of suffering, *no matter the face of expression reproduced.*

FAITH BOUIE

How you choose to perceive what is true for you will shape the reality that you see in accommodation to what is held to be true inside. This is a common philosophy that is known by many. And it is true for the very means of how you perceive suffering. Indifference is born from the belief that *you are not something*. Consequently, you are rejecting yourself as you neglect what you see out of the fear of it *actually* being you, and revealing to you the very thing that you need to see.

Great wisdom is gained from the expression of all things as you, and as you honor your pain as yourself truly, you are enlightened and exposed to the true beauty which lies so seemingly hidden within the expression of what is felt as *discomfort*. You are an epitome of transmutation in the dimple of reality as you allow for the ongoing fluctuations of energy (which are you in disguise) in your garden of presence and *absence* of control.

Chapter VI

COMPASS ION - An Introduction To Conscious Meditation

October 12th, 2019

THE GATEWAY TO YOU

Y*ou are the deliverer of greatness upon the physical plane* as creative consciousness instilled into various expressions of physical form, matter, thoughts, feelings, senses, and emotions. You are the grand decipherer and translator of all things, as well as, the very decryption and translation of all which is perceived. You are the creator as *you are creation.*

How you perceive all things as yourself determines your reception of the principle.

What we perceive as the many common features of life are essentially codes of energy, as consciousness serves as the very space in which all manifestation is born into *realization.*

The wisdom of who you truly are lies within the very space which is indicated here, which is why simply cherry-picking out only certain favorable things within your reality and acknowledging them as your own can be very limiting to the grander truth of who you are.

An *already existent you* stands as the void to that which all reality is born into existence.

What is thus presented to you as "reality" becomes the residual aftereffect to what has already taken place upon subtler realities of you. It is matter and vibration which are products from the workings of a subtler platform of you, vibrating at a separate rate and course of frequency. To this greater effect, the philosophy that *all things are you* thus becomes the gateway model for the ultimate discovery of self as light consciousness and creation upon all realms and platforms of hidden and conscious reality.

Compass Ion is a model that identifies the reasoning behind why things are manifested as they are presented within reality. And this realization behind why things are how they are lies beyond the common negotiations of ego ponder and deduction. As ego observes reality it regurgitates thoughts that are formatted within the same interpretation of that reality. *The act of thinking thoughts* initiates this process, while *the reception of knowledge* reflects a relaxed, intuitive and ever more dilated mind within alignment with the greater course in which things flow into fruition.

How you observe and interact with reality as it transpires within *the comprehension of all things as yourself truly* can be achieved within the practice of Compass Ion. The concept can be understood as two separate theorems: *Compass*, which represents the collective noise of creation expressed as vibration, and *Ion*, which is acknowledged as the absence and presence of frequency.

It is *frequency* which determines the presentation of vibration.

While *Compass* reflects form and vibration, *Ion* represents the frequency at which energy vibrates. And to this effect, the notion behind why things present how they do becomes Ion, as the vibration that is perceived in reality thus functions as *Compass*.

***

THE EXCLUSION OF SELF AND A CONSCIOUS MIND

As consciousness is realized upon the face of vibration, the regard of *"self"* and identity gracefully melts into the greater totality of creation quite naturally. With little to no effort on your part, there lies only one necessary shift in your awareness from the mind into feeling. However, the feeling is not the feeling that we commonly regard as emotion. The feeling that is indicated here is a feeling which sits within the trunk of the body as an eternal flux of continuous sensation. It is this sensation which represents consciousness expressed within the denser impression of form, for consciousness can take many faces of expression upon the various planes of our reality. And to this effect, consciousness is felt as one creates this shift from mind into basic bodily perception. As mind relaxes and dilates to the alignment of consciousness, the thoughts produced become secondary to that of consciousness. And *a conscious mind* results from this natural phenomenon.

The mastery of Feeling is another philosophy to be discussed in a later channeling within the overall series; however, it is important at this time that it is briefly introduced in the very initial steps of self disillusionment.

***

CONSCIOUSNESS AS THOUGHT

Shifting your awareness from mind into the subtle expression of consciousness which sits within the trunk of your body allows mind its natural place in the true order in which things come into incarnation, and so accordingly are all subsequent thoughts thereby manifested as derivatives to that of conscious perception. Once this is achieved, messages are revealed in the true natures in which they are meant to be received.

***

RECEIVING TRUTH

The reception of truth is reliant on your scale of trust in the presence of what emerges into consciousness through mind. What is more, from the premise that all things are essentially you, we want to avoid the discard of anything that may seem as counterintuitive referring to how you may have once perceived yourself in the past because what you truly are lies beyond *and* among reality as the many things hidden and seen.

Reception begins with the dilation of mind and the perception of consciousness. Once these steps are achieved consciousness floods the mind naturally as truth becomes an intuition received in the presence of consciousness. In the presence of consciousness, thoughts surfaced within mind are accompanied with and without emotional charge. Emotional charge is a healthy by-product of thought which arises within the body as communication. When emotions are received in the absence of ego and presence of consciousness, a transmutation thus transpires as reception initiates the metamorphosis of what was once perceived as emotion. How you proceed with what is revealed to you is to your discretion.

COMPASS ION - *All Things You Model*

Perceiving all things as yourself begins with the observation of what is here now before you. You can choose anything that you would like to begin with, be that a person, place, object, or thing. As you clear any indication of doubt within the mind, the natural shift of awareness will follow the proper course into the feeling which subsists within the body as eternal sensation. This feeling presents subtly in the presence of ego; however, as your mind relaxes in dilation and preparation for receiving, the feeling will grow into awareness and become more apparent to you as this transpires.

You flip the switch of reality as the latter is achieved, and life becomes a secondary exhibit to the expansive nature of you.

***

Let us use the common door handle as an example of the practice of self as all things. By simply observing a door handle, you may quickly come to notice its color, shape, and size without a second glance. That is all that you need in the swift deduction it is indeed a door handle. Mind stops at this point as it is thus satisfied with the notion of it being a door handle, which is a necessary process in the overall recognition of one's self in reality.

Subsequently, once ego is pacified, a simple suggestion to the possibility that the door handle *is not* a door handle leaves enough room for the reanalysis of what is there. The frequency of the door handle can be perceived through conscious perception as mind dilates to its natural state. And as you hold awareness to the door handle, the frequency of consciousness felt within the body shifts to match that of the door.

***

Classifying frequency is not the objective here as consciousness can be perceived in its own intelligence in the absence of thought. Your true objective is to simply acknowledge the feeling present within the body as you regard the door handle. And the practice is thus complete.

Now let's say that you were to hold the same regard to a particular person within your life. The process would unfold in the same light; however, the result would fare differently for you. As you watch the people around you, your mind classifies what it perceives via names, race, gender and/or occupation to just name a few. It enjoys the process of categorizing people into separate files of classifications for easier comprehension.

Let's take another example such as the photo of a friend. It is a natural reflex of the mind to quickly provide the name of whom you are observing. Allow this to happen, and as you do, simply observe any other accompanying thoughts and/or emotions that may arise in context to what is observed.

Once the mind has successfully reached a state of agreement, simply suggest the possibility that the person in the photo is not the details that were concluded. For instance, a simple suggestion would reflect a question such as, *"What if Joe wasn't Joe?"*. This would be more than enough to trigger the mind into reception-mode. Instant recognition takes place as your consciousness matches the frequency of the person within the photo, and you may even find that emotions are ever more inclined to arise at this time, as well.

Perchance an overwhelmingly compassionate gaze may suddenly overcome you in the absence of thought, as the reception of truth is thus revealed to you through the intelligence of pure consciousness.

The message is received at this time, and the practice is concluded.

***

Chapter VII

Conscious Meditation

October 18th, 2019

CLOSING REGARDS TO CONSCIOUS MEDITATION

Conscious meditation is the meditation of life as it unfolds before you. Choice opens this practice by simply acknowledging how one interacts within his reality. Reaction versus conscious reflection is to be regarded here, for there exist only two faces within the perception of life experience: *feeling prompted into reaction and feeling prompted into conscious reflection in the absence of thought.*

This reflection can feel much more uncomfortable than the mere *quick and easy* reaction. Consciousness holds a physical presence upon the physical plane within the trunk of your human system, and this sensation more than often bottles very uncomfortable, emotional vibrations held knotted within suppression.

This is why so many of us flee from the body, because repressed emotions are stored here as well. Mapping consciousness upon reality can therefore only be achieved as one remains receptive to the consciousness present within the body.

Life can be activated within the true light of its greatest potential as one's perception shifts from defaulted action into the consciousness perceived within the body as life transpires.

***

It's simple. The goal is for you to observe something before you while perceiving consciousness within the trunk of your system simultaneously. Instead of turning directly to the mind for immediate assistance, *as many of us do*, you would rather turn to the sensation that is felt within the body while holding observation to what is there. In achieving this, your mind will follow by principle, and all thoughts which follow will be those that are founded in truth. It is this Feeling (consciousness) that *precedes* the thought. And as this is achieved, thought follows within the proper course of manifestation.

Trust becomes the major principle here. For as you trust in *what is felt* upon your observation of reality, much more can be perceived at a more rapid and expansive rate of comprehension. What is more, the faculties of subconsciousness are stimulated here as one dwells within the pure consciousness of what is being perceived in the absence of ego.

***

You can complete this exercise anywhere at any time, which is the very beauty of conscious meditation. There lies no need for you to close your eyes (although it may certainly enhance the experience), for the importance here relies upon the utilization of the senses and common practices of life-interaction.

As one's response to life shifts in this respect, what was once perceived as ego will no longer be perceived. This is because the origin of mind's *desire to know* is satisfied upon the soul's recognition of consciousness upon the body, and in its place, another voice thus emerges to consciousness when appropriate in the unfoldment of expression upon many planes of reality.

***

Seeing all things as yourself truly as reality is perceived is the very first principle of conscious meditation upon life within the *Compass Ion* series of channelings. Following the principles of conscious meditation whilst observing reality as yourself bridges light consciousness unto the physical, and compassion is born from a viable source of truth.

May these teachings help to guide you along your own personal journey to spiritual enlightenment.

Until next time. Namasté

FAITH BOUIE

ABOUT THE AUTHOR

Faith Bouie is an author and certified clinical hypnotherapist. Her work is channeled from an altered state of consciousness following deep reflection and meditation. She is a graduate of the Institute of Interpersonal Hypnotherapy and is a member of the International Association of Interpersonal Hypnotherapists. She holds over 500hrs of extensive training in hypnotherapy, including Parts Therapy, Age-

FAITH BOUIE

Regression, Neurolinguistic Programming (NLP), Eye Movement Therapy, Breathwork, and many more powerful transformational modalities. In addition to her writing, she is a nurse and musician. She has practiced the art of classical violin for over 10 years, with notable performances at the Van Wezel Performance Hall in downtown Sarasota and Carnegie Hall in New York City. She enjoys meditation, tarot, and yoga outside of her work, as well.

www.ingramcontent.com/pod-product-compliance
Lightning Source LLC
Chambersburg PA
CBHW031455040426
42444CB00007B/1112